THE STRATEGIC PLANS OF
LIBERAL DEMOCRATS

BY PAUL BURKE

ILLUSTRATED BY KENT GAMBLE

Binary
PUBLICATIONS

The Strategic Plans of Liberal Democrats

Paul Burke ~ Kent Gamble

BINARY PUBLICATIONS LLC

**THIS BOOK IS PUBLISHED IN TWO VERSIONS.
DEMOCRATIC & REPUBLICAN**
(why should we limit ourselves to 50% of the buying public?)

Research:
Hua Yu
Rick LeMoyer
LeMoyer Rick
M.Y. Opinion

Data Aggregators:
Buzz Teilowell
Cyd E. Street

Editor:
Petunia Powers

Information Regulator:
Loui Burke

DEDICATION

The authors wish to dedicate this book to Section 107
of the doctrine of Fair Use in the United States Copyright Law
and all the privileges it grants to the creative community.

"We all do better when we work together. Our differences do matter, but our common humanity matters more."
William J. Clinton

"The nine most terrifying words in the English language are, 'I'm from the government and I'm here to help.'"
Ronald Reagan

"Coming together is a beginning.
Keeping together is progress.
Working together is success."
Henry Ford

The Strategic Plans of Liberal Democrats

The Strategic Plans of Liberal Democrats

The Strategic Plans of Liberal Democrats

The Strategic Plans of Liberal Democrats

The Strategic Plans of Liberal Democrats

The Strategic Plans of Liberal Democrats

The Strategic Plans of Liberal Democrats

The Strategic Plans of Liberal Democrats

The Strategic Plans of Liberal Democrats

The Strategic Plans of Liberal Democrats

The Strategic Plans of Liberal Democrats

The Strategic Plans of Liberal Democrats

The Strategic Plans of Liberal Democrats

The Strategic Plans of Liberal Democrats

The Strategic Plans of Liberal Democrats

The Strategic Plans of Liberal Democrats

The Strategic Plans of Liberal Democrats

The Strategic Plans of Liberal Democrats

The Strategic Plans of Liberal Democrats

The Strategic Plans of Liberal Democrats

The Strategic Plans of Liberal Democrats

The Strategic Plans of Liberal Democrats

The Strategic Plans of Liberal Democrats

The Strategic Plans of Liberal Democrats

The Strategic Plans of Liberal Democrats

The Strategic Plans of Liberal Democrats

The Strategic Plans of Liberal Democrats

The Strategic Plans of Liberal Democrats

The Strategic Plans of Liberal Democrats

The Strategic Plans of Liberal Democrats

The Strategic Plans of Liberal Democrats

The Strategic Plans of Liberal Democrats

The Strategic Plans of Liberal Democrats

The Strategic Plans of Liberal Democrats

The Strategic Plans of Liberal Democrats

The Strategic Plans of Liberal Democrats

www.ingramcontent.com/pod-product-compliance
Lightning Source LLC
Chambersburg PA
CBHW080533030426

42337CB00023B/4716